YOUR KNOWLEDGE HAS VALUE

Bibliographic information published by the German National Library:

The German National Library lists this publication in the National Bibliography; detailed bibliographic data are available on the Internet at http://dnb.dnb.de .

Imprint:

Copyright © 2015 GRIN Verlag, Open Publishing GmbH
Print and binding: Books on Demand GmbH, Norderstedt Germany
ISBN: 9783668218994

This book at GRIN:

http://www.grin.com/en/e-book/322774/luhrmann-s-when-god-talks-back-under-standing-the-american-evangelical

Timothy McGlinchey

Luhrmann's "When God Talks Back. Understanding the American Evangelical Relationship with God". A Critical Reflection of her Findings and Approach

GRIN Publishing

GRIN - Your knowledge has value

Since its foundation in 1998, GRIN has specialized in publishing academic texts by students, college teachers and other academics as e-book and printed book. The website www.grin.com is an ideal platform for presenting term papers, final papers, scientific essays, dissertations and specialist books.

Visit us on the internet:

http://www.grin.com/

http://www.facebook.com/grincom

http://www.twitter.com/grin_com

Religion and Ritual Book Review:

When God Talks Back: Understanding the American Evangelical Relationship with God

T.M.Luhrmann

I intend to introduce this essay in the same way Tanya Luhrmann (2012) introduces her book; with perhaps some of the most intriguing and pertinent questions that challenge both the modern day understanding of religion, and indeed, the anthropologists who study it. How are rational, sensible people able to sustain belief in an endlessly powerful, yet completely invisible God, in an environment of overwhelming scepticism? And, how does this God become real for these people? Luhrmann sought to answer these questions through long-term ethnographic fieldwork amongst evangelical Christians, more specifically, congregants of the Vineyard churches across America. In this essay I will seek to summarise and critically engage with the theories Luhrmann developed, the findings she made, and importantly, the approaches she used in the formation of her book: When God Talks Back. In doing so, I hope to shed more light onto the field of the anthropology of religion by exploring the broader applications of her work.

For more than two years, Luhrmann immersed herself in the life of the churches she attended, and in many ways, became as much a member as any other. She went to countless Sunday morning services, was part of Bible study groups, involved herself in any practices or events held by the church, and even saw a spiritual director. This being said, she was far from passively participating. During the course of her fieldwork she interviewed dozens of Vineyard congregants, recorded services and Bible studies, and had church members take part in her own qualitative and quantitative questionnaires and tests. Fundamentally, she was seeking to understand the intricate elements, purposes and effects of faith and faith practices, and did so from her own perspective as a cognitive anthropologist. My conclusion to Luhrmann's findings is that the persistence of Christianity, in the face of scepticism, is explained by the personal reality of God that congregants come to experience through constructing what she has defined as a "participatory theory of mind" (2012:40). In brief, this refers to the method of perceiving, and discerning between, the external world and one's internal thoughts and feelings, in a way that allows one to experience God whilst working around the barriers imposed by modern day scepticism. In this essay I will focus on explaining this theory and providing examples of the experiences it provokes, whilst also exploring some of the practices involved in attaining this new theory of mind. Throughout, I will analyse the benefits and drawbacks of the approaches adopted by Luhrmann, namely cognitive and functionalist, questioning their effectiveness in contributing to the field of the anthropology of religion.

When first introducing the "theory of mind", Luhrmann suggests that it is a cognitive mechanism everyone uses as a means of separating and discerning between what happens externally in the physical world around us, and what happens within the privacy of our minds. However, Luhrmann's claim is that the faith of the charismatic Christians of the Vineyard church requires a new theory of mind. This theory must

2

accommodate for a God who is not only intimately familiar with one's inner, private world, but can even interact with it. She suggests that this framework is established through the Christian practices and teachings of churches as well as the intentional efforts of the individual. This sentiment is clearly explained when she posits, "The task of becoming a Christian… demands that one set out deliberately to overcome this fundamental human awareness that our minds are private" (2012:40). She specifically defines this achievement as the "participatory theory of mind" (ibid), as it insists on the barriers between mind and world being "porous" (ibid) and accepting of God. This, therefore, leads to a new process of interpreting internal processes, and external events, which actively involves and incorporates God.

Luhrmann's cognitive approach is clearly active here in that she seeks to explain how culturally produced practices can deeply influence the psychological dynamics linked to religious adherence. This notion is clearly reflected by the influential cognitive anthropologist D'Andrade, in discussing the effectiveness of this approach; "Another major accomplishment [of the cognitive approach] has been to provide a bridge between culture and the functioning of the psyche" (1995:252). In assuming Luhrmann is correct, that a new theory of mind is indeed developed through the practices that some Christians attend to, then it appears to surface in a variety of different ways. Although it is crucial to investigate how such a mind-set is formed, perhaps it is more important to first understand how it manifests itself for these Christians, as these experiences are crucially interwoven throughout the major focuses within the book. Despite there being numerous unique examples of such experiences,

3

in general I see them as falling within several key categories of subjective interpretation; internal processes such as thoughts and feelings; external events; and "sensory overrides" (2012:216).

To explain the case of internal processes, I will use the example provided by Luhrmann of Elaine, a Vineyard congregant. We are told that Elaine, at one point, decided to become a missionary in Africa because she had a "vivid dream about being on an African safari" (2012:275). A dream appears to be a common medium through which Christians interpret God as speaking to them. The new theory of mind, as Luhrmann would argue, comes into play here as it allowed Elaine to experience the dream, not just as a dream about Africa, but as a message or even direction from God that she should be doing missionary work there. In the case of interpreting external events, Elaine's case is once again applicable. The book is rich with testimonies and examples of when God has revealed things to people through very real occurrences such as conversations, sights and "coincidences". In Elaine's case, very soon after she had her dream, she was in a Sunday service and found herself talking with someone she did not previously know, Ann, with whom she felt a "deep connection" (ibid). That person gave Elaine a pamphlet relating to ministry which she realised she had dreamt about, "that very booklet, with that cover" (2012:276). In this case, Elaine's new theory of mind led her to interpret this external incident, not as a friendly yet insignificant encounter, but as God solidifying her existing belief that He was directing her towards ministry and mission. The term "sensory overrides" is one that is generously scattered throughout Luhrmann's research and refers to fairly rare experiences where one's senses are hindered, almost tricked, in an involuntary way and are believed, by the subject, to be real as opposed to mis-remembered; as she explains, "They are experienced as the sensory perception of something external" (2012:216). David, another Vineyard congregant, is a prime example for the occurrence of sensory overrides. He said that sometimes he would see things as real in the world in front of him, and that he has even felt God touch him. The apparent reality of such events for people, like David, who experience them, does seem to support the validity of a cognitive approach to understanding experiences of the divine, resulting in what feel like very real encounters.

Moreover, having dissected some of the most relevant manifestations of the proposed "participatory theory of mind", it is now important to critically engage with the claims Luhrmann makes and analyse whether the cognitive approach she used is truly helpful in contributing to our general understanding of religion. In my opinion, the theory is effective at explaining one, albeit key, element of religious experience, whilst ignoring another. It provides a very strong explanation for why Christians who believe in God and wish to experience Him can come to do so, but to a large extent ignores the multiple accounts of non-Christians who have had very similar "religious" experiences (that have led to a change in belief) but who have had neither the desire, nor the spiritual direction to construct this new theory of mind. Although it is within the framework of Luhrmann's research to exclusively investigate how Christians come to experience God, if the theory is to account for any widespread cognitive explanation of such experiences, then non-believers should, in my opinion, also be considered. This being said, simply because experiences of non-Christians do not feature highly within Luhrmann's research, does not render the entire theory invalid, at worst it renders it unfalsifiable, and at best, incomplete.

Otherwise, I consider her cognitive approach extremely beneficial in exploring the world of an evangelical Christian, and more specifically, their perception of that world. In describing the role of the cognitive anthropologist, D'Andrade says, "The cognitive anthropologist studies how people in social groups conceive of and think about the objects and events which make up their world..." (1995:1). Considering this, I would suggest Luhrmann's new theory of mind accounts for the framework through which the Vineyard congregants perceive their world.

However, before any final conclusions can be drawn, it is crucial to analyse the theory in full, and to do so, one must understand its construction. One of the first things that Luhrmann stresses about the theory is that it is not instantaneous and does require time and external influence. As she explains here, "These evangelical Christians, then, not only have to accept the basic idea that they can experience God directly; they must develop the interpretive tools to do so in a way that they can authentically experience what feels like inner thought as God-generated" (2012:41). There are many ways in which these "interpretive tools" are developed, I wish to focus on several: church-led emotional practices and "Let's Pretend" play.

Firstly are the church-led emotional practices, of which, Luhrmann identified six, and although I will not dwell on them all individually, she recognised each one as significant and recurring amongst congregants. These practices are; crying in the presence of God; seeing from God's perspective; practicing love, peace and joy; God as therapist; reworking God the Father; and emotional cascades. Each practice is a means through which members of the Vineyard church come to experience God and grow in their relationship with Him further. Interestingly, from Luhrmann's perspective, she likens these practices to a form of psychotherapy. She suggests that the ultimate goal of therapy is to make the client feel loved, or at least lovable, and within churches, these therapeutic conditions and practices focus on God's love of the congregant; "in a church, these practices are different from ordinary psychotherapy because the 'therapist' is more powerful than any human therapist and also more perfect" (2012:111). Although this claim still remains cognitive in its nature, it also contains functionalist elements in that it gives God a function, making the congregant feel loved.

The concept of pretending is also a prominent and recurring theme throughout the book. The chapter, "Let's Pretend" begins by saying that the first task in coming to experience God is learning to recognise Him in one's own mind, and the second task is learning how to relate to God as a person. The title is based on a quote from C.S. Lewis' Mere Christianity (1952) - "Let us pretend in order to make the pretence into a reality" (2012:73). By this Luhrmann is not suggesting that the Vineyard congregants pretend that God is real, whilst believing otherwise, but instead pretending is seen as a practice through which they can come closer in their relationship with God. Such pretending practices exceed simply acknowledging the presence of God with you and

7

in you, but in fact physically demonstrating this belief. This manifests itself in various forms such as what some congregants refer to as "date night". In this "pretence", women would set aside a night to have a meal with God where an extra plate will be laid out and chair put in place, and as she puts it, they "imagined their way through the evening talking to God, cuddling with God, and basking in God's attention" (2012:80).

This notion of pretend also finds itself in other aspects of Christian practice such as in prayer. In the case of Hannah, another member of the Vineyard church, she told Luhrmann that her ability to hear God speak had become much more vivid since learning to imagine God as a person by her side. She prayed to God about everything and treated him as a friend, and that was what he became; "Let us pretend in order to make the pretence into a reality" (2012:73). In referring to popular Christian book which talks about experiencing God, Luhrmann quotes one particular line, "The crisis of hope that afflicts the church today is a crisis of imagination" (2012:84). Such books and ideologies in general prioritise seeing God as a person, a friend, before recognising Him in the light theology and even understanding. It is this that leads Luhrmann into her first major concern of the "Let's Pretend" principles – it lacks the margin for error that is needed when interpreting a God as complex and incomprehensible as the God of Christianity. Their main concern is not that God will be imagined falsely, but that He will not be imagined at all. Returning to the participatory theory of mind in relation to this discussion, it would appear that the experience of God remains the most influential factor, beyond simply the knowledge of Him.

Having now explored some of the key practices that contribute to the formation of the participatory theory of mind, it is important to critique the conclusions made as well as the effectiveness of the approaches used in reaching them. With regards to the notion of God as a therapist and church-led emotional practices as psychotherapy, I would suggest that the functionalist approach is a useful addition in that it perhaps fills the gap left by a cognitive approach. One drawback of the cognitive approach is that while it provides logical answers to the question of how certain practices are effective in constructing the new theory of mind, to some extent it leaves out the question of why? To perceive these practices as functional brings an element of reason to the theory. However, the functionalist approach is also open to criticism. One major, and recurring, fault within the approach is that the function, or awareness of it, cannot precede the existence of the practice as this would imply that the practice's development anticipated its function. With the case of God as the therapist, the belief in God preceded the emotional practices involved in faith which acted as a form of therapy, therefore, although those practices might have a therapeutic function, it is the result of the emotional practices, not the cause of them. I feel the approach also neglects to recognise the importance of individual actors and the process of interaction - different people respond differently to the same practices. For example, one of the practices mentioned was crying in the presence of God, and this was seen as therapeutic. However, although many did cry during prayer and faith practices, not everyone did, therefore the function is not always applied.

As for the cognitive approaches used in explaining the practices, I would say that they are largely helpful in explaining the construction of the theory of mind. One frequent criticism of cognitive approaches to anthropology the investigator can be guilty of arriving at conclusions that are not reflective of how individuals really do perceive society. This probably roots from the fact that the culture contained in the mind is difficult to analyse objectively. This being said, considering how immersed Luhrmann became in the culture of evangelical Christianity, and the emphasis she placed on basing her findings on what she was told by those she studied, this perhaps reduces the potency of the criticism. Similarly, Geertz once criticised cognitive approaches for loading too much meaning into practices (1975:12). Although this may certainly be the case with many claims from the perspective of cognitive anthropology, in Luhrmann's case most of the meaning that has been inferred from practice is supported by other relevant research or interviews with congregants and therefore taken from the source of the practices.

To conclude, Luhrmann set out to answer two fundamental questions; how are rational, sensible people able to sustain belief in an endlessly powerful, yet completely invisible God, in an environment of overwhelming scepticism? And, how does this God become real for these people? I would claim that the answer in fact lies in the questions. It is through experiencing God as real that one can come to believe in him in the face of overwhelming scepticism. Or as the American Philosopher William

James put it; "God is real since he produces real effects" (2008:3374). The processes that build the new theory of mind for the Vineyard congregants are intentionally experiential, whether it's "date night" with God, or the intensity of sensory overrides. Through such practices these evangelical Christians can come to experience a reality that is drastically different to the reality of those who have not experienced God, as Luhrmann elegantly puts; "They live in the same world and yet in very different worlds" (2012:300). And so, through the divisive use of the cognitive approach to the anthropology of religion, and the support of functionalist elements, Luhrmann has succeeded in delving deep into the lives of these Vineyard congregants to identify and explain what the reality of God looks like to them.

Bibliography

D'Andrade, R. (1995) *The Development of Cognitive Anthropology*. Cambridge: Cambridge University Press

Geertz, C. (1975) *The Interpretation of Cultures*. London: Hutchinson

James, W. (2008) *The Varieties of Religious Experience: A Study in Human Nature*. Rockville: Arc Manor

Lewis, C.S. (1952) *Mere Christianity*. London: HarperCollins

Luhrmann, T.M. (2012) *When God Talks Back: Understanding the American Evangelical Relationship with God*. New York: Alfred A. Knopf

YOUR KNOWLEDGE HAS VALUE